children's room
essentials

JUDITH WILSON

children's room
essentials

RYLAND
PETERS
& SMALL
LONDON NEW YORK

ST. MARY'S ROAD BRANCH

Designer Emilie Ekström
Senior editor Henrietta Heald
Picture research Claire Hector
Production Deborah Wehner
Art director Gabriella Le Grazie
Publishing director Alison Starling

10 9 8 7 6 5 4 3 2 1

Some of the text in this book first
appeared in *Children's Spaces*

First published in the United Kingdom
in 2004 by Ryland Peters & Small
Kirkman House
12–14 Whitfield Street
London W1T 2RP
www.rylandpeters.com

Text copyright © Judith Wilson 2004
Design and photographs copyright
© Ryland Peters & Small 2004

A CIP record for this book is available from the British Library.

ISBN 1 84172 684 2

Printed and bound in China.

contents

bedroom styles

babies' rooms   8
girls' rooms   14
boys' rooms   22
shared rooms   30

living spaces

play spaces   40
eating spaces   48
bathrooms   54

suppliers   60
credits   61
index   64

bedroom

styles

Right This nursery storage unit was specially built by a carpenter. The cupboard has a pull-out changing surface and a box to hold baby wipes, plus shelves for nappies.
Opposite If you combine proper cupboard storage with easy-access shelves, toddlers can easily get hold of their favourite things.
Below Scaled-down furniture is a friendly as well as a practical part of a toddler's bedroom.

babies' rooms

A baby needs little in the early days, although department stores might try to persuade you otherwise. Many infants don't even move into their own rooms until three months or beyond, perfectly content to swing in a cradle at their parents' bedside. Nevertheless, a new arrival does need its own bedroom, for nappy changing, storing clothes and to house a nascent collection of toys.

The main nursery basic is a cot. Simple styles are both practical and chic. More enticing than traditional varnished pine are beech or cherrywood, white-painted wood, colourful lacquered MDF or ironwork. A cot bed, with slatted sides that are removed as the baby grows up, is a cost-effective option.

A padded bumper protects restless little heads, but choose one in plain colours and with quilting, not frills. Cotton sheets and blankets and a comforting quilt are the other basics. When your baby is two years old, add a baby pillow and cot duvet. Blankets and sheets now come in every colour. Pick and choose between different coordinated ranges, or add a retro piece or two.

The area for changing nappies should be efficient and fuss-free. Don't bother to buy a specialist unit, which will soon be redundant. A chest of drawers at the correct height, with a plastic padded mat on top, can double as a changing area. Store all the essentials – nappies, wipes and creams – in the drawers immediately beneath, or place them on a chunky MDF shelf above the chest yet still within arm's reach. If you have room, consider a custom-made unit. You will need alcoves for clothes, cotton wool, nappies and so on, with a pull-out or pull-down changing surface.

A low, comfortable armchair is a must for feeding. Get a loose cover made in a sturdy, washable fabric – bright denim, robust linen or towelling. If there's room, beanbags in jelly-bean colours or wipe-clean vinyl cubes are great for babies learning to sit up or crawl.

Whitewashed walls and a neutral floor make the ideal backdrop for colourful accessories. But if you (and your baby) need stimulation, paint one wall in a bold shade such as cherry red or swimming-pool turquoise. If you prefer soothing pastels, stronger tones such as lavender or duck-egg blue make the best background for primary-coloured toys. Try painting abstract shapes: stripes or giant dots look good. Don't forget the ceiling – babies spend hours on their backs.

String the ceiling with Chinese lanterns, party bunting or paper mobiles. You don't have to cover the walls with pictures, but you and baby need something lovely to look at.

Opposite, left Simple embroidery can be used to give cot sheets or pillowcases a personal touch.
Opposite, right Take advantage of natural light by putting a cot under a window, but make sure that you have a blind or curtain that is efficient enough to exclude glare.
Below and left In a baby girl's nursery, a whitewashed antique cot sets the tone for a simple yet pretty room. Pastel-painted peg rails hung with tiny dresses brighten white walls, and an ever-changing display of nostalgic pictures, family snaps and paintings means that there is always something stimulating for the baby to look at.

Above Bright colours and abstract shapes make a baby's room more stimulating. The low armchair is a comfortable place for feeding.
Above right The double divan with surround on a tubular frame is ideal for a toddler who has outgrown a cot but is not yet ready for a bed.
Opposite Not all babies have the luxury of their own room. A cot in a corner of the parents' bedroom can be individualized in small decorative ways, with lengths of colourful bunting, for example.

Use imaginative lighting to add a creative dimension. If there's an overhead light, fit it with a dimmer switch, essential for checking on the baby at night. Plunder both adult and children's lighting departments for unusual options. As well as 'magic lantern' children's lamps, which splash the walls with gentle colour and movement, consider a lava lamp, strings of flower fairy lights, illuminated globes or punched-metal lampshades that cast patterns.

You'll probably need more space for baby clothes than you expect. Little vests and sleepsuits make quite a pile, then there are gifts of clothes waiting to be worn, as well as outgrown garments. A wardrobe isn't essential. Instead, choose a generous chest with plenty of drawers, which can be updated with a coat of paint or contemporary handles. A giant laundry basket is a must for a fast turnover of clothes. Wicker baskets, zinc tubs or colourful plastic crates stacked on shelves or tucked beneath the cot will all make tidying easy.

- Plain **painted** walls create the most **restful** ambience in a baby's **first** room.

- Keep things simple with **clear** colours, **quick-access** storage and a stimulating view from **the cot**.

- Sensory touches add **magic** – perhaps a **wind chime** or twinkling fairy lights.

- Anticipate the **crawling** phase by keeping blind cords short, trailing cables clipped and **socket covers** on.

Far left A swathe of fabric with a slot heading adds sophistication to a simple metal bed frame.
Left This painted lampstand has a decorative as well as a practical function, combining fun and order.
Below left The striking lime walls, purple rubber flooring and a scarlet spotty-dotty bedcover are very appealing to young taste.
Opposite Fitted storage does not have to mean cupboards. The high platform bed in this teenager's bedroom incorporates plenty of large drawers. The wall-mounted TV shelf also saves on floor space.

girls' rooms

Most little girls love pretty things. But give your daughter a break from the classic flowery bedroom and offer her instead a fresh, contemporary take on the feminine look. Crisp fondant colours or an all-white room make the perfect background for little girls to display their special treasures. For tomboys, more subdued shades and quirky, abstract patterns are appealing.

Below right A Victorian day bed, with decorative open ironwork, makes an attractive bed choice for older girls. It looks particularly romantic draped with a fabric canopy or mosquito net.

Below Girls love to admire their clothes, so provide space to line up shoes, plus low hooks for hanging up hats and party dresses.

When a toddler turns two and graduates from a cot to a bed, it provides a timely moment for reassessing the bedroom and making stylistic changes. Focus first on the hard-working furniture, planning colours later. Invest in the best mattress you can afford. Children may be light but they need firm support, and a good-quality mattress should last for ten years. Think long and hard about the style of bed you choose. Girls will go through myriad fads, from Barbie-doll fever at five to seriously sophisticated at ten. Work backwards. If a classic style with a contemporary twist seems suitable for a pre-teen, it can be made appropriately childlike for the earlier years.

Canopied and four-poster beds, bunk beds or sleeping platforms prove irresistible to girls, as well as providing extra space for sleepover friends. A simple wood or tubular metal four-poster offers plenty of decorative potential. Frames can be draped with brightly coloured net one year, home-made strings of shells the next, or with inexpensive, glittery sari silks for older girls. A platform bed can usefully accommodate storage or a desk beneath, and for stylistic continuity can be custom-made in materials used elsewhere in the house. Practical plywood, painted MDF or galvanized steel are all options, and will be softened with colourful bed linen and teddies. Just as little girls love to choose their dolls' clothes,

Above and above left A metal bedstead is a good investment, since it can be restyled from year to year or resprayed in a new colour. Hunt down antique ones in junk shops. A bed head at each end has its advantages, providing somewhere to pile up pillows and to hang bags and toys. An older girl will appreciate plenty of open storage. Here, toys, schoolwork and treasures are all to hand.

they'll relish the chance to mix and match pillowcases and duvet covers. Provided they are from a complementary palette, crisp checks, plains and florals mixed with white will look great jumbled together on the bed. Extras such as an embroidered pillowcase, cosy travel blanket or appliquéd top sheet make the final effect more individual.

The bed may be top priority, but storage comes a close second. Plan for, or with, your daughter by writing a list of everything she needs to keep in her bedroom, from toys and clothes to decorative inessentials. Not everything has to be put away at all times, but each item should have a home.

If the room is large enough, the smartest and simplest storage option is to fit a run of cupboards with floor-to-ceiling, flush-fitting doors along one wall. Behind this façade you should provide a multitude of different-sized

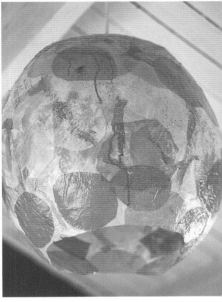

shelves, roomy enough to hold individual crates for small items yet deep enough for piles of sweaters and jeans, and including space for a hanging rail. Open shelves may seem a tempting option for finding toys at a glance, but closed doors look neater.

Ideally, you should provide an area for your little girl to draw and do her homework. Take a tip from contemporary interiors and provide her with a long, low worktop with wall-mounted shelves above. It could be painted MDF or covered in stainless steel or colourful laminate. Site the computer here; beneath the bench, fit crates on castors for toys or books, a second stool for a friend,

Above Create a dramy, tranquil atmosphere with pretty lighting such as paper globes, Chinese lanterns or a mini chandelier.
Above left Young sisters may prefer sharing a low double bed with two duvets rather than having single beds at opposite ends of the room.
Left Don't assume girls want a fairy grotto. This little girl's bed, with its seafaring theme, has delighted her since her toddler years.
Opposite A custom-made platform bed in painted MDF or plywood is a brilliant space saver as well as creating a cosy, self-contained unit.

even a cabinet with lots of shallow drawers for colouring pens and paper. If you add a mirror, a worktop can also double as a dressing table and display space.

Most children relish a colourful environment and will want to be involved in choosing their favourite shades. Follow the same rules as you would anywhere else in the house. Jolly brights like sherbet yellow or cornflower blue are stimulating, but use them on a single wall so the effect isn't overpowering.

Remember that your daughter's room is her private haven, a place for chats with friends, somewhere quiet to do homework, a retreat for dreaming and scheming. Help her to delineate her territory from other siblings so she can be alone when she chooses. You could mark her door with a giant gilded initial, for example, or get a metalwork company to cut out her name in stainless-steel letters.

Left Nothing beats open cube shelves for quick toy storage. Fit some with cupboard doors so that messier items can be concealed.
Right Include scaled-down pieces, such as tiny chairs. Pick light, easy-to-move designs, so that girls can rearrange them during play.
Above right Mini shopping bags provide impromptu storage.
Opposite Children enjoy the cosy sloping ceilings of an attic room, but it can be hard to squeeze in conventional furniture. Commission a carpenter to custom-build shelves and cupboards under the eaves.

• Painted walls rather than **wallpaper**, display space for treasured **accessories** and classic furniture all make for a **relaxed**, easy bedroom.

• Just as little girls love to choose their **dolls' clothes**, they'll relish the chance to **mix and match** pillowcases and duvet colours.

• For a girl who likes privacy, create a **hideaway**. String suspension wire between walls to **divide off** the bed area, and add a voile curtain.

• Little girls love to display **treasures**, so provide a good, generous shelf or table top for all those **papier-mâché** models, beach shells, sparkly **tiaras** and family photos.

boys' rooms

Boys care passionately about their bedrooms. From around the age of five, most of them know instinctively what accessories and motifs are 'cool' and will want to incorporate at least some into their private space. They may fuss less than girls about an overall scheme, but are obsessive when it comes to the smaller details. What boys need most is empty floor space – as much as you can spare – and plenty of storage so that their myriad collections, from toy soldiers to racing cars, can stay well ordered and ready for play.

Left A bunk bed is an excellent option for a boy's room. Your son can sleep on the safe lower level until about the age of six, and graduate to the higher level when he feels ready for it.

Above and opposite Choose quirky, vibrant colours for a bright, trendy boy's room. Wall-mount as much furniture as possible, leaving space for all the essentials of the boy zone – a football table, dartboard, punchbag or basketball hoop.

Everything in a boy's room should be robust. Imagine each piece of furniture being jumped off, climbed on or moved around as part of a pirate ship game or impromptu kickabout, and you'll get a realistic picture. Pick scratch-resistant modern materials like laminate and plywood, or painted furniture that can be easily touched up with a lick of paint.

Boys still require a cosy sleeping nook at the age of three, but by five are ready for a more adventurous, classically boyish option. Either buy a generously sized cot bed for the baby stage and get a serious boy's bed once your son outgrows the cot or invest in a grown-up bed at the age of two, and make it inviting for the early years.

Boys, as much as girls, appreciate a fuss being made over their bed. It does not simply represent somewhere to sleep, but is a child's special secure zone as well as being a potential platform for imaginative games. Ready-to-buy modern options might include sophisticated dark wood or painted bateau-lit and sleigh-bed frames, simple iron bedsteads or colourful lacquered MDF platform beds with storage drawers. For most boys past the age of five, a bunk bed is a dream option. A number of shops now stock tubular metal bunk beds, which are infinitely more stylish than the varnished pine variety.

A platform bed frees up more floor space for playing, so is a boon in a small room. Storage cupboards, a generous run of

Left In this toddler's bedroom, a high picket-fence headboard, a faux-fur rug and thick, tufted curtains promote a safe, cosy feel.
Below Furniture on castors and bright plastic storage crates that can be slotted under the bed are invaluable in a small room.
Opposite, left As an alternative to dog-eared posters, consider a bold painted canvas depicting your son's favourite sporting hero.
Opposite, right Brilliant, saturated colour on every surface, from walls to furniture, transforms an ordinary bedroom into an entertaining playroom. Here, the startling walls are matched by equally vibrant bed linen – a riot of crazy stripes, animals and exotic fruit.

worktop or, with a lower bed, lots of pull-out drawers, can be variously incorporated underneath. Make furniture on castors a theme – everything from a chest of drawers to a low play table. Even better, clear the floor with wall-mounted shelves for books, baskets for miscellaneous bits and pieces, hooks for clothes and even ceiling-suspended seating – perhaps a hammock or a swinging pod chair.

Most boys have little interest in putting clothes away, so devise a simple storage system. Open shelves in a cupboard are the easiest option, but clearly label each section for T-shirts, jeans and so on. Alternatively, build a series of box-shaped cupboards at child height all around the room, with

each one devoted to a certain category of clothing, and fitted with a different-coloured MDF or stainless-steel door to resemble a sports locker. Give your son a row of child-height hooks where he can hang up his pyjamas or anything else that has been strewn across the floor. Don't expect him to line up his shoes neatly. Instead, provide one big basket, and agree that this is the designated place for all shoes at tidy-up time.

Little boys play constantly on the floor, so flooring should be hard-wearing and attractive as well as providing a smooth surface. There's nothing more frustrating than trying to race

Below left A custom-built bed maximizes space in a small room, and adds quirky charm. And little children are less likely to fall out of beds that are boxed in or have high sides. Storage can be incorporated in the form of under-bed drawers.
Below and opposite page Detailing counts for just as much in a child's bedroom as it does in a grown-up space. Ornaments should be fun and colourful, and boys should have plenty of space to show off treasures. A shelf unit can be the decorative centrepiece of a room, and it needn't always be spotlessly tidy. Children love anything that spells out their name. Letters on the door lend an air of importance, as does anything monogrammed.

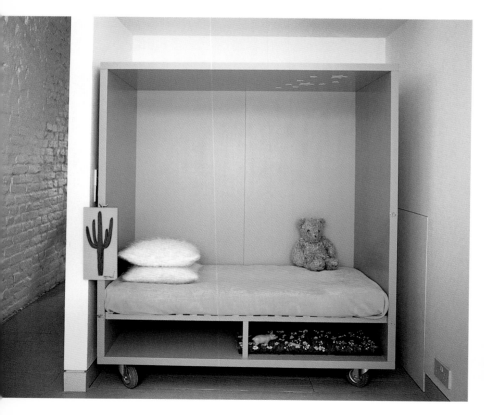

cars along badly sanded wooden boards, or to arrange army platoons on bumpy sisal matting. Far more practical, and infinitely smarter, are painted or waxed wooden boards, wood laminate flooring or brightly coloured rubber tiles.

If your son is mad about a cartoon character, indulge his passion with a giant floor cushion made up in appropriate fabric or a big poster, then ignore further demands. Crazes come and go, and next year he will have moved on to another phase. If you create a neutral canvas with plain painted walls and a white roller blind, you can introduce any theme.

Boys may be boisterous and busy, but there are times when they want a special area in their bedroom for relaxing and being with friends. If there's no room for a sofa, give your little

Right Low hooks provide quick access to clothes. Look out for decorative, themed designs, but ensure pegs are long enough to hold clothes securely.

Below Built-in storage and a bed all along one wall free up play space. With bedding stored in big drawers beneath it, the bed can be used for somersaults or sitting with friends.

Opposite Mixed with simple wooden furniture, a collection of old-fashioned toys creates a nostalgic bedroom. Use one piece to inspire a decorative theme: mix a sailing boat with nautical stripes, or tin soldiers with camouflage motifs.

boy the chance to turn his bed into a lounge-lizard spot. He will enjoy touchy-feely fabrics on the bed. Keep duvet covers and sheets in strong plains and add a pure wool checked blanket. A giant fleece-fabric blanket in a vivid hue such as scarlet or grass green looks neat tucked over the duvet by day. A cut-up old sleeping bag, made into squishy cushions, is also fun. Give boys a chance to create their own ambience in the room using lighting – a bubble lamp by the bed, a light-up globe on the desk or a funky coil of lights are all good options. Try to squeeze in a few quirky additions. A football table, punchbag or wall-hung basketball hoop will make your son's room the coolest den he could ask for.

- For boys, aim to create a **cool den** that's fuss-free and has versatile **furniture** for **imaginative** play.

- Raid the **colour spectrum** for inspiration – scarlet, leaf green, **indigo** – then team with robust surfaces such as **rubber** and **wood**.

- For toys, the **ideal** storage system combines plenty of **small drawers**, crates or boxes with **bookshelves**.

- A **steel** pinboard, equipped with magnets, is a great place to display **school art work** and certificates.

shared rooms

Plenty of children share a bedroom. As a parent, you may anticipate only the downside of this arrangement: disrupted bedtimes, arguments over territory, one child wanting to study while the other chooses to chat. But it needn't be a nightmare. Ask any grown-up who shared a room to recall childhood memories, and many will remember the fun of reading by torchlight after lights-out or the pleasure of two sets of toys. Besides, for a child to wake up with his or her siblings and fall asleep with them each night is a great gift.

Left and opposite One way to approach a room shared by a boy and a girl is to keep the basic units unisex. Here, polished boards, metal cupboards and metal-legged beds provide a neutral background. Give each child's area a distinct character by using the bed and wall behind it as a focal point.
Below This room for older boys takes a shared dormitory as its theme. White shutters, plain floorboards and utilitarian metal-framed beds all suggest summer camp, while the furniture – a battered sports locker, individual initialled trunks and aluminium chairs – completes the look.

Children sharing a bedroom will find it fun to have a formal division of territory, so that during arguments or when entertaining friends each can retreat to their private zone. First, decide if the division will be visual or physical. For little ones, the less physical separation the better. They will derive comfort at night by having their beds close together, and reading a joint story will be simpler for you.

If your children get on well, divide up the room space into separate sleeping, play and work zones instead of two distinct areas with bed, chest and so on. Bunk beds or sleeping pods on a shared platform can be divided from the play space with a sliding screen or curtains. The children can either share one long countertop to do homework or have two identical desks side by side.

When a boy and a girl share, you will need to reconcile two definite and differing tastes. For little ones, paint walls white or choose a bold shade, then personalize each child's bed. There's nothing more charming than two identical bedsteads side by side, but characterize each with different duvet covers: an identical design, perhaps, but in two contrasting colours. Take the theme a step further, and colour-coordinate each child's bedside table, rug and lampshade.

When same-sex siblings are sharing, you can easily indulge all-girl fantasies or all-boy passions. But you still need to personalize the two-of-everything accessories, so that sharers are clear about who owns what.

Far left Two divans placed at right angles, with a shared, sturdy cube side table, is a comforting and sensible option for small children. **Left and below** Bunk-bed styles, in minimal tubular steel or ready-to-paint MDF or are ideal for a shared room, and perennial favourites with children, perhaps because they double as climbing frames. If there is a playroom elsewhere in your house, a shared room can be kept ultra-simple.

Some children are messy, while others are neat, so to avoid arguments over tidying give each child his or her own chest of drawers, shelves or wardrobe. A bedside table for each, to hold a night-time drink, books and lamp, is also essential. Since shared rooms frequently double as playrooms, ensure that everything can be tidied away quickly and hidden behind closed doors.

If you have picked a stimulating decorative scheme, flexible lighting is one way to calm things down at bedtime. In shared rooms, the right lighting is especially important. Different-aged children may have staggered lights-out times, so that while an older child needs a task light for reading in bed, a younger sibling might need a glowing nightlight. For playtime, low-voltage ceiling lights provide brighter illumination than a single overhead pendant, but fit them with a dimmer switch.

Above right One way to resolve the issue of kids with differing tastes is with a dominant mural, which can negate the need for boundaries. It makes the room that contains it everyone's room – a magical place to go to sleep and wake up.
Right Each child needs somewhere to keep special toys. Provide a 'secret' box for under the bed, or agree that toys placed on a certain chair must not be touched.
Opposite In this shared all-girls room, the symmetry of side-by-side sleigh beds and twin chairs creates a tranquil ambience.

When children enjoy sharing a bedroom, it becomes a real den, their own private space versus the family house. If space permits, give them a daybed or an inflatable chair to lounge on, and consider installing a TV for older kids. If there is a younger sibling who doesn't share, and everyone is in agreement, the daybed could be used at weekends for sleepovers so the little one can join in the fun. Likewise, give each child who shares the chance to sleep alone occasionally, in a spare bedroom or on the sofabed. Children, like adults, need some time away from the fray.

- Siblings who share need clearly marked **personal zones**, their own private corners and **decoration** that they both **adore**.

- **Kit out** the room with two of everything, then create a **fun environment** that's ideal for shared play and midnight **feasts**, yet serene enough for soothing bedtimes.

- A colourful **fantasy mural** will appeal to both sexes, but try to keep shapes **simple** and the look graphic.

a bedroom is ...

Children, just like **adults**, need privacy, so give them **freedom** to enjoy **time out** in their **individual** bedrooms.

Kids will like being **involved** in a room scheme they can be **proud of** - and will be more likely to keep the room **neat**.

a child's private space

Plan bedrooms that are fun for **little friends**, with seating to chill out on, or a futon for **sleepovers**.

Adopt a five-year plan, and anticipate each **new** need, from a work desk to **funky furnishings** for pre-teens.

living

spaces

play spaces

Every child needs space to play. An expanse of floor, a freshly cleared tabletop and enough room to race around are the essentials. As adults, we allocate ourselves activity zones – a sofa to sprawl on, a desk for paying bills – and children need their own equivalent. Size should not be the issue; whether it's a patch of floor in a kitchen or dining room, or a separate playroom, what's important is that this is an area that children can call their own. If you make toys accessible and easy to tidy away, your kids will even enjoy organizing their own private zone.

Opposite, left A wooden or MDF desktop, fixed on an adjustable rack system, provides a corner for quiet play or drawing and writing.
Opposite, right Experiment with the shelving levels, especially in a small space. Shelves can be run around a room at ceiling height, hung below a window or wall-mounted.
Left Tall shelving units can serve kids' and adults' needs alike. Dangerous or precious items, or infrequently used toys and books, can be stored well out of the way, while lower shelves are devoted to everyday necessities.
Below Look out for gadgets that keep play equipment neat inside a cupboard: stacking boxes, plastic CD racks and a wooden paper dispenser are all good options.

Above Don't feel obliged to keep everything small – the best dens will appeal to adults too. Choose squashy beanbags, a wall-size blackboard or a big chill-out sofa.

Opposite, left A low custom-made bench, teamed with a freestanding play table and chairs, makes a cosy place for adults and children in the playroom. Design one with a lift-up lid, so there is more storage inside.

Opposite, right In a large playroom, try to incorporate desk space for older children, for doing homework or using a family computer.

There are many advantages to an open-plan living space. Tiny children can safely play under a grown-up's watchful eye while cooking, watching a video or DVD and older kids' homework all get under way. If you are moving house to accommodate a growing family, this is the ideal space configuration to aim for. It is helpful to have a toilet nearby, so little ones don't have to travel too far from their toys. And, if possible, access from the living area/play space to a garden or safe roof terrace is invaluable.

If you can't move house but are adapting your living quarters to suit children, think long and hard about the changes you make. You will reap the benefits of employing an architect, although it may seem expensive at the time. An architect will think laterally about maximizing space and can squeeze storage into the most unlikely corners. Alternatively, if finances are tight, can rooms be swapped around? Perhaps a dining room off the kitchen could be made into a playroom? But if you have a spare room away from the living area that might be converted into a separate playroom, think twice about doing so when your children are small. You don't want to be cooking with half an ear on what's going on next door, and life is easier if you don't have to call a halt to exciting play in one room and move children to the kitchen to eat.

The disadvantage of sharing a space with kids is that they bring a sea of bright plastic with them. Provide effective storage so that toys can be put away quickly and grown-up order restored. One solution is to equip the space with floor-to-ceiling cupboards with flush doors and deep shelves. Put kids' things on the lower shelves and household items on the upper ones. If you can, specify extra-deep cupboards so that fold-up dolls' buggies or plastic garages can fit in easily. If open shelves are the only option, invest in containers that look good en masse.

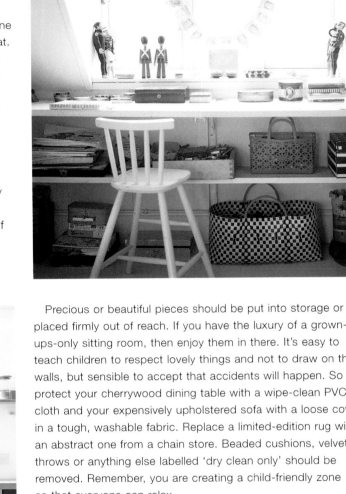

Precious or beautiful pieces should be put into storage or placed firmly out of reach. If you have the luxury of a grown-ups-only sitting room, then enjoy them in there. It's easy to teach children to respect lovely things and not to draw on the walls, but sensible to accept that accidents will happen. So protect your cherrywood dining table with a wipe-clean PVC cloth and your expensively upholstered sofa with a loose cover in a tough, washable fabric. Replace a limited-edition rug with an abstract one from a chain store. Beaded cushions, velvet throws or anything else labelled 'dry clean only' should be removed. Remember, you are creating a child-friendly zone so that everyone can relax.

The beauty of integrating kids' stuff with contemporary design is that trendy industrial-style surfaces like stainless steel, plywood and laminate are smart and hard-wearing, and the clear, bright colours of much modern furniture are enhanced when littered with toys. Walls in white vinyl matt emulsion create a simple background but you can have fun with colour too. A single wall in dazzling bright blue can look stunning, particularly if decorated with children's artwork.

Polypropylene chairs are a practical, easy-clean option and 1960s-style versions in vivid tangerine or lime green are great fun. If a table doubles as a dining and painting table, a wipe-clean surface is essential, so a laminated top is perfect. To house a video or DVD machine, choose a long cabinet rather than open shelves. Have a steel one powder-coated in pink, and make a design statement

at the same time. You can also be imaginative when selecting fabric for the playroom sofa or chairs. Several bright plains can create an abstract effect if used as blocks of colour on individual chairs, seats and cushions. Patterned fabric is good for disguising sticky finger marks. When decorating a play space, you can be a little tongue-in-cheek. A 1970s swivel chair upholstered in Mr. Men fabric would look suitably funky, as might a giant abstract painting that blurs the barriers between modern art and kids' naïve efforts.

Every play area should have a cosy corner for watching a video or DVD, or listening to music. If space permits, a small sofa is wonderful for after-lunch naps or quiet reading; if there is not enough room for this, beanbags work equally well. Play spaces in communal living areas often have hard floors, perhaps wood or limestone, so a rug or a fluffy faux animal-print throw provides a softer sitting or crawling area for babies and toddlers.

Above A freestanding, floor-level bookshelf is ideal for small children, making books simple to stack.
Above left Shallow drawers are excellent for organizing pens, paper and art materials. Look out for a play table with an integral drawer, or plastic drawer units on wheels.
Opposite, left The best storage is both practical and good-looking.
Opposite, right Deep drawers hold plenty of toys and are easy for children to reach. Be imaginative with the drawer fronts: cut out patterns from MDF or choose stainless-steel or wooden fascias.

play spaces should allow ...

Modern **flooring** materials such as concrete make the **perfect** surfaces for toy trains and cars.

Every **play space** needs comfortable low-level seating for relaxing in front of a video or **reading**.

the imagination to roam

Put art equipment and **materials** in low cupboards or **on open shelves**, so kids can have **easy access** to them.

Stainless steel, wood, **laminate** and painted MDF offer **hard-wearing** play surfaces that **clean up** efficiently.

eating spaces

Children's mealtimes may resemble lunchtime at the zoo, but if you choose practical equipment and furniture at least it shouldn't take long to clean up. Babies progress rapidly from being spoon-fed to helping themselves in a highchair and then graduating to the grown-ups' table. Whatever stage your children have reached, the process of getting them to sit down, eat calmly and observe table manners needs to be achieved with minimum fuss and maximum efficiency.

Opposite, left Miniature table and chair sets need not be clumsy pieces of moulded plastic in garish colours. For an individual and stylish look, choose more elegant versions that mimic grown-up contemporary classic styles.

Opposite, right In a large multifunctional kitchen, plan to retain a generous area of floor space, so that small children have plenty of room to run around – then group together the activity zones for intimacy and practicality. Children like perching on chairs close enough to chat to parents while they prepare food.

Left and below In a corridor-style kitchen, even the smallest table makes the room user-friendly for children.

If possible, put a children's dining table in the kitchen, so you can keep an eye on the kids while preparing food or clearing up. Don't despair that your high-tech contemporary kitchen will be spoiled by highchairs and brightly coloured crockery. Colourful seating, a lime-green toaster or pink plastic beakers will only pep up the stainless-steel cabinets.

A highchair is essential for babies. Standard designs are practical but can be an eyesore. Better-looking ones include simple wooden Scandinavian designs or plain white lacquered steel versions. Or look for a second-hand highchair, repaint it in a bold colour and re-cover the seat in a retro-print oilcloth. A sturdy canvas or plastic clip-on seat is sociable for older babies, because it fixes onto the tabletop.

Little ones often like to have a diminutive table and chairs at which they can eat meals or draw and paint. But, if you like to sit with the kids while they eat, you may not find it very comfortable. Eating at a breakfast bar or adding a low countertop to the end of an island unit might be a better solution. The sooner you encourage small children to sit up at the adults' table, the better, but if you have a beautiful table, protect it with a PVC cloth at all times.

Polypropylene, metal or wood chairs are good for family mealtimes. Pick a style that is comfortable and safe for children as well as looking smart. School-style benches are also excellent, offering extra room for friends.

Left The combination of a breakfast zone on a worktop and a separate dining table means that homework or drawing needn't be cleared away when meals are served.
Below If planning a kitchen/dining room from scratch, choose units with children's needs in mind. This kitchen looks slick, but is in bright, fun shades. Storage for tableware has been cleverly combined with shelves for art materials and books.
Opposite An island unit makes the ideal breakfast bar for slightly older children: a 25 cm (10 inch) overhang on the worktop gives sufficient leg-room. Furnish it with high stools, which children love.

With imaginative shopping, you and the children will find laying the table positively creative. Tiny versions of anything will delight them, and a choice of colours is great, because each can pick his or her favourite. Not everything has to be plastic, though dayglo picnic sets are a good source of plates and cups. Duralex glass tumblers are virtually indestructible and come in appealingly small sizes. Many casual dining ranges are in robust pottery, and traditional enamel plates and cups are also hard-wearing.

Everything to do with kids' mealtimes should be accessible for them, as it encourages setting the table from an early age. Store bowls and cutlery in a low cupboard and drawers and keep lunchboxes in there too. Is the fridge easy for an older child to open, so they can help themselves to snacks? Is there a sturdy stool for a little one to hop onto so he can get a drink of water from the tap? The easier you make eating and drinking for your children, the sooner they will be integrated into the sociable world of family mealtimes.

make meals fun ...

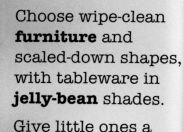

Choose wipe-clean **furniture** and scaled-down shapes, with tableware in **jelly-bean** shades.

Give little ones a diminutive **table** and chairs at which they can eat meals or **draw** and paint.

Mix and match **tableware** to make meals more lively. Add jolly **accessories**, from funky cutlery sets to a retro, tomato-shaped **sauce dispenser**.

Pick **robust**, easy-mop flooring: laminate, **sanded** and painted timber boards, vinyl, bright rubber and **limestone** are all **practical** choices.

with vibrant eating spaces

bathrooms

The bathroom is one of the most hard-working spaces in the home. It must be efficient enough for the before-school wash and brush-up yet cosy enough to prompt fun-filled bathtimes. Most children have a love–hate relationship with their daily ablutions. One week, they will obsessively brush their teeth; the next, they are frightened of the shower. But nearly all little ones find it soothing to wallow in a bath.

Left If space allows, double basins make perfect sense in a shared bathroom. Allocate one basin to the children, with a shelf for novelty soaps and toothbrushes. Provide steps so that little ones can stand at the right height.
Right Bathtime is much more fun for children if the bathroom has decorative touches that appeal to their imagination, such as these low shelves for bubble bath and toys.
Opposite Sealed or painted wooden boards are suitable for a children's bathroom, but wood laminates are sensitive to deluges of bath water.

When planning a bathroom from scratch, first decide whether to have a bath and separate shower cubicle or a shower attachment wall-mounted over the bath. Little ones generally prefer baths to showers but may slip if they shower standing up in the bath. If an over-bath shower is the only option, buy a non-slip rubber mat and a groovy plastic shower curtain.

To cope with the early morning rush, two (or even three) basins make sense. There are plenty of stylish, practical choices that are ideal for kids. Small stainless-steel bowls set into a stone or wood worktop look ultra-trendy, as do wall-hung white ceramic butler's sinks. A small basin designed for cloakroom use is another option.

Cross-head or lever taps are much easier to handle than slippery, minimal round knobs, while a mixer tap will guard against hot scalds. A counter with inset washbasin provides ample space for washroom essentials. But if the basin is freestanding, fit the tooth mug into a wall-mounted holder, so it can't be knocked over, and replace slippery soap bars with liquid soap in a neat chrome dispenser. A wall-hung toilet can be sited slightly lower than usual. Consider whether a push-button flush mechanism would be better than a stiff handle.

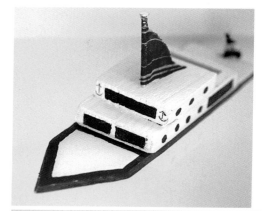

Left Rolltop baths are good for children, since they have no sharp edges. Reconditioned Victorian baths often come in small sizes.
Below Efficient storage is essential in a shared bathroom. This one has under-sink cupboards as well as out-of-reach units for adult use.
Opposite page Kitsch plastic items such as bright fish, toy boats and rubber dinosaurs make a children's bathroom more fun. Add a narrow shelf above the bath for display, or group objects along a windowsill.

If you make your bathroom 100 per cent splashproof now, you won't mind about water fights later. Fun floor options include non-slip rubber tiles in bright colours, linoleum or vinyl. Cork floor tiles with PVC laminate finish also come in water-themed designs such as sand and shells. Sealed or painted wooden boards are also suitable. Stone, such as limestone or slate, is smart and waterproof but it gets slippery when wet, so invest in an absorbent bath mat.

Floor-to-ceiling tiles are a sensible idea for the walls. In a children-only bathroom, big, square tiles in a cheerful shade look graphic and modern. For a coordinated look, colour-match them with laminate worktops or a painted wooden floor. Walls can also be lined with tongue-and-groove or MDF panels. Paint them and the walls in eggshell, which resists condensation and splash marks. If sanitaryware is white, have fun with colour on the walls. Jazzy shades such as grass green and turquoise are particularly appropriate.

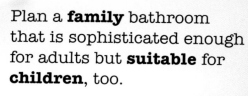

Plan a **family** bathroom that is sophisticated enough for adults but **suitable** for **children**, too.

Surfaces must be **robust** and easy to clean. Vividly hued laminates make good **bath panels** and surrounds, while stone, from **limestone** to slate, is practical and **stylish**.

make your kids' bathroom ...

Plan plenty of storage for bathroom **paraphernalia**, including a high **lockable cabinet** for any medicines.

Provide a big **plastic bin** so that toys can be tidied away **easily** after bathtime.

a tempting place to be

suppliers

BED LINEN

Couverture
310 Kings Road
London SW3 5UH
020 7795 1200
www.couverture.co.uk
Children's collections, hand-
made babies' blankets and
vintage pieces.

Damask
3–4 Broxholme House
New Kings Road
London SW6 4AA
020 7731 3553
www.damask.co.uk
Cot and bed quilts in pretty
florals or appliquéd designs.

Descamps
197 Sloane Street
London SW1X 9QX
020 7235 7165
www.descamps.com
Whimsical children's cot and bed
linen with matching bedspreads,
nightwear and bathrobes.

Designers Guild
267–71 Kings Road
London SW3 5EN
020 7351 5775
www.designersguild.com
Bright animal- and flower-print
bed linen with coordinating fabrics
and accessories.

Laura Ashley
Call 0871 230 2301 or visit
www.lauraashley.com
Co-ordinating fabrics, bed linen and
ready-made curtains featuring
flowers and truck motifs.

Mothercare
Call 08453 304030 or visit
www.mothercare.com
Colourful cellular and fleece baby
blankets, coordinating bedding
ranges and nursery furniture.

The White Company
261 Pavilion Road
London SW1X 0BP
0870 900 9555
www.thewhitecompany.com
Solid wood furniture, decorative
bed linen, children's nightwear,
bedroom accessories and
babywear.

FURNITURE

Argos
0870 600 1010
www.argos.co.uk
Cheap and cheerful children's
furniture, including bed linen,
beds and fun accessories.

Back in Action
11 Whitcomb Street
London WC2H 7HA
020 7930 8309
www.backinaction.co.uk
Children's chairs and tables, plus
furniture to help good posture.

Chic Shack
77 Lower Richmond Road
London SW15 1ET
020 8785 7777
www.chicshack.net
Painted children's furniture,
including cots, beds and
storage, in 18th-century French
and Swedish styles.

The Conran Shop
81 Fulham Road
London SW3 6RD
020 7589 7401
www.conran.com
Good storage options, plus mini
versions of classic chair designs.

Habitat
Call 0845 6010 740 or visit
www.habitat.net
Metal bunk beds, melamine desks
and wardrobes, beanbags and
miniature table and chair sets.

Heal's
Call 020 7636 1666 or visit
www.heals.co.uk
Contemporary children's furniture
and accessories, including wooden
bunk beds with storage beneath.

IKEA
Call 0845 355 1141 or visit
www.ikea.co.uk
Inexpensive, flat-packed modern
bunk beds, desks, storage units,
miniature tables and chairs, plus
lots of fun accessories.

lionwitchwardrobe
020 8265 8449
www.lionwitchwardrobe.co.uk
Beautifully designed contemporary
solid wood furniture for children.

Mufti
789 Fulham Road
London SW6 5HA
020 7610 9123
www.mufti.co.uk
Beautiful bespoke children's
furniture, including scaled-down
four-poster beds, leather chairs
and desks.

Next Home
Call 08702 435435 or visit
www.next.co.uk
Metal bunk beds and bright
beanbags, plus funky bed linen,
shower curtains and storage items.

Oreka Kids
020 8804 2045
www.orekakids.com
Manufacturers and suppliers of
Biscuit plywood children's furniture,
including fun folding tables.

Stokke UK
Call 01753 655873 or visit
www.stokke.com
Manufacturers and importers of
the Scandinavian Tripp Trapp chair,
which grows up with the child.

The Swedish Chair
020 8657 8560
www.theswedishchair.com.
Swedish-style painted wooden
cots, adjustable high chairs
and beds.

MAIL ORDER CATALOGUES

Aspace
01985 301222
www.aspace.com
Sleek and simple children's
beds, chests of drawers and
wardrobes.

The Children's Furniture Company
020 7737 7303, www.thechildrens
furniturecompany.com
Beautifully designed children's beds
and storage, in beech or coloured
veneers, featuring interchangeable
engraved motifs, including trains.

The Great Little Trading Company
0870 850 6000
www.gltc.co.uk
Imaginative children's furniture,
accessories and gadgets, plus
personalizing service.

Urchin
Call 0870 720 0709 or visit
www.urchin.co.uk
Practical and contemporary furniture,
accessories and gadgets for trendy
babies and kids, from mobiles to
beanbags and fun tableware.

Wigwam Kids
0870 902 7500
www.wigwamkids.co.uk
Attractive contemporary furniture
for babies, girls and boys.

Win Green
01622 746516
www.wingreen.co.uk
Bunting, cushions and beanbags
in bright plains and ginghams.

BEDS

Bed Bazaar
The Old Station
Framlingham
Suffolk IP13 9EE
01728 723756
www.bedbazaar.co.uk
Specialists in reconditioned
antique beds; also mattresses
in unusual and small sizes.

Bump
020 7249 7000
www.bumpstuff.com
Several styles of ready-to-paint
MDF sleigh beds, including
bunk-bed and daybed versions.

Harriet Ann Beds
Cherry Garden Farm
Hastings Road
Rolvenden
Cranbrook
Kent TN17 4PL
01580 243 005
Great selection of antique wooden
sleigh beds. Mattresses and small
sizes available, or original designs
made to order in reclaimed pine.

The Iron Bed Company
Call 01243 578888 or visit
www.ironbed.com
A good selection of iron
bedsteads, including hand-
painted sunflower designs.

STORAGE

The Holding Company
241–45 Kings Road
London SW3 5EL
020 7352 1600
www.theholdingcompany.co.uk
Ingenious baskets, boxes, bags
and hanging racks.

Muji
Call 020 7323 2208 or visit
www.muji.co.uk
Good selection of steel
shelving as well as cardboard
and acrylic storage boxes.

FABRICS/WALLPAPERS

Cath Kidston
51 Marylebone High Street
London W1U 5HW
020 7229 8000
www.cathkidston.co.uk
Simple florals in pretty colours,
with matching oilcloth and retro
children's fabric cushions.

John Lewis
Oxford Street
London W1A 1EX
020 7629 7711
www.johnlewis.com
A good source of inexpensive
ginghams and plain cottons.

Lena Proudlock/Denim in Style
01666 500051
www.deniminstyle.co.uk
Suppliers of denim fabric in more
than 50 colours, plus large and
small beanbags.

The Natural Fabric Company
mail order:
PO Box 163
Banbury
Oxon OX15 6ZX
www.naturalfabriccompany.com
Basic fabrics, with plain cottons,
checks, ginghams and denims.

BATHROOMS

C P Hart
Newnham Terrace
Hercules Road
London SE1 7DR
020 7902 1000
www.cphart.co.uk
Wide range of contemporary wall-
hung sinks and baths in every size.

First Floor
174 Wandsworth Bridge Road
London SW6 2UQ
020 7736 1123
www.firstfloor.uk.com
Stockists of Dalsouple rubber
floor tiles, lino and vinyl tiles.

Pipe Dreams
72 Gloucester Road
London SW7 4QT
020 7225 3978
www.pipedreams.co.uk
Scaled-down toilets and basins in
any finish, including glittery pastels.

ACCESSORIES

Made
020 8960 6969
www.made.co.uk
Funky sheepskin beanbags and
rugs in bright plains, plus designs
including cherries and dogs.

Mathmos
22–24 Old Street
London EC1V 9AP
020 7549 2700
www.mathmos.co.uk
Contemporary lighting, including
the original lava lamp.

The Rug Company
Call 020 7229 5148 or visit
www.therugcompany.info
Contemporary and traditional
floor coverings.

SKK
34 Lexington Street
London W1F OLH
020 7434 4095
www.skk.net
Trendy lighting, including paper-
bag-style lamps and paper string
lights in heart or flower designs.

Urban Outfitters
36–38 Kensington High Street
London W8 4PF
020 7761 1001
Kitsch accessories, including funky
shower curtains and sparkly lamps.

credits

Key: ph = photographer, a = above, b = below, r =r ight, l = left, c = centre.
Photography by Debi Treloar unless otherwise stated.

Endpapers & **1** ph Caroline Arber/G-rumpy bear by Jane Wellman, cushions by Caroline Zoob; **2–3** Vincent & Frieda Plasschaert's house in Brugge, Belgium; **4l** Architect Simon Colebrook's home in London; **4a** Imogen Chappel's home in Suffolk; **5** Clare and David Mannix-Andrews' house, Hove, East Sussex; **6–7** Imogen Chappel's home in Suffolk; **8l** ph Christopher Drake/Diane Bauer's house near Cotignac; **8r** An apartment in London by Malin Iovino Design; **9** Kate and Dominic Ash's home in London; **10l** ph Caroline Arber/Caroline Zoob; **10r** ph Caroline Arber/ Emma Bowman Interior Design; **11** Victoria Andreae's house in London; **12l** Clare and David Mannix-Andrews' house, Hove, East Sussex; **12r** Ab Rogers & Sophie Braimbridge's House, London, designed by Richard Rogers for his mother. Furniture design by KRD–Kitchen Rogers Design; **13** Vincent & Frieda Plasschaert's house in Brugge, Belgium; **14** Kate and Dominic Ash's home in London; **15l** Designed by Sage Wimer Coombe Architects, New York; **16–17** Cristine Tholstrup Hermansen and Helge Drenck's house in Copenhagen; **18** Michele Johnson's home in London designed by Nico Rensch Architeam; **19a** House by Knott Architects in London; **19b** The Boyes' home in London designed by Circus Architects; **20l** New build house in Notting Hill designed by Seth Stein Architects; **20r** Cristine Tholstrup Hermansen and Helge Drenck's house in Copenhagen; **21** Architect Simon Colebrook's home in London; **22–23** Sera Hersham-Loftus' house in London; **24b** Kristiina Ratia and Jeff Gocke's family home in Norwalk, Connecticut; **24a** Sudi Pigott's house in London; **25a** Victoria Andreae's house in London; **25b** Kate and Dominic Ash's home in London; **26l** Family home, Bankside, London; **26r** & **27** Sudi Pigott's house in London; **28a** Julia & David O'Driscoll's house in London; **28b** Belén Moneo & Jeff Brock's apartment in New York designed by Moneo Brock Studio; **29** ph Caroline Arber/Emma Bowman Interior Design – cushion Caroline Zoob, quilt Housepoints; **30–31** Eben & Nica Cooper's bedroom, the Cooper family playroom; **31r** Ben Johns & Deb Waterman Johns' house in Georgetown; **32–33** An apartment in New York designed by Steven Learner Studio; **33a** Ian Hogarth's family home; **33b** New build house in Notting Hill designed by Seth Stein Architects; **34b** ph Caroline Arber/Sharland & Lewis, rabbit from Lizzie's; **34a** Pear Tree Cottage, Somerset, mural by Bruce Munro; **35** Sue & Lars-Christian Brask's house in London designed by Susie Atkinson Design; **36al** Suzanne & Christopher Sharp's house in London; **36bl** The Boyes' home in London designed by Circus Architects; **36br** Sarah Munro and Brian Ayling's home in London; **37l** Wim and Josephine's apartment in Amsterdam; **37ar** ph Christopher Drake/Marisa Cavalli's home in Milan; **37br** Catherine Chermayeff & Jonathan David's family home in New York, designed by Asfour Guzy Architects; **38–39** David & Macerena Wheldon's house in London designed by Fiona McLean; **40l** An apartment in London by Malin Iovino Design; **40r** Family home, Bankside, London; **41l** A family home in Manhattan, designed by architect Amanda Martocchio and Gustavo Martinez Design; **42** A family home in London; **43l** Architect Simon Colebrook's home in London; **43r** Cristine Tholstrup Hermansen and Helge Drenck's house in Copenhagen; **44l** Ian Hogarth's family home; **44r** Belén Moneo & Jeff Brock's apartment in New York designed by Moneo Brock Studio; **45l** ph Caroline Arber/artist Jessica Zoob's family home in London, chair and table from Housepoints; **46a** ph Caroline Arber; **46b** ph Caroline Arber/The Arbuthnott family's house near Cirencester designed by Nicholas Arbuthnott, interior design and fabrics by Vanessa Arbuthnott, eiderdown Sharland & Lewis, samplers Carla Marx; **46–47** Sarah Munro and Brian Ayling's home in London; **47ar** Ian Hogarth's family home; **48l** Designed by Sage Wimer Coombe Architects, New York; **48r** Catherine Chermayeff & Jonathan David's family home in New York, designed by Asfour Guzy Architects; **49** A family home in Manhattan, designed by architect Amanda Martocchio and Gustavo Martinez Design; **50** Kristiina Ratia and Jeff Gocke's family home in Norwalk, Connecticut; **51l** Family home, Bankside, London; **51r** Designed by Ash Sakula Architects; **52bl** Paul Balland and Jane Wadham of jwflowers.com's family home in London; **52r** A family home in London; **52ar** The Swedish Chair – Lena Renkel Eriksson; **53l** Designed by Sage Wimer Coombe Architects, New York; **53br** Architect Simon Colebrook's home in London; **54** Ben Johns & Deb Waterman Johns' house in Georgetown; **55** Robert Elms and Christina Wilson's family home in London; **56l** Vincent & Frieda Plasschaert's house in Brugge, Belgium; **56r** ph Caroline Arber/Hoggy & Mark Nicholl's home in Wiltshire, decorator John Nurmington, Malmesbury; **57b** Vincent & Frieda Plasschaert's house in Brugge, Belgium; **58al** Ben Johns & Deb Waterman Johns' house in Georgetown; **58bl** Paul Balland and Jane Wadham of jwflowers.com's family home in London; **58r** Fifth Avenue Residence, New York City designed by Bruce Bierman Design, Inc.; **59l** Sophie Eadie's home in London; **59br** Ab Rogers & Sophie Braimbridge's House, London, designed by Richard Rogers for his mother. Furniture design by KRD–Kitchen Rogers Design.

architects and designers whose work is featured in this book

Amanda Martocchio, Architect
189 Brushy Ridge Road
New Canaan, CT 06840
USA
Pages **41l**, **49**.

Asfour Guzy Architects
+ 1 212 334 9350
easfour@asfourguzy.com
Pages **37br**, **48r**.

Ash Sakula Architects
www.ashsak.com
Page **51r**.

Brian Ayling, Artist
020 8802 9853
Pages **36br**, **46–47**.

Bruce Bierman Design, Inc.
www.biermandesign.com
Page **58r**.

Bruce Munro
Mural commissions
01749 813 898
brucemunro@freenet.co.uk
Page **34a**.

Caroline Zoob
Textile artist and interior design
01273 479274 for commissions
Caroline Zoob's work is also
available at:
Housepoints
020 7978 6445
Pages **1**, **10l**, **29**.

Christina Wilson, Interiors Stylist
christinawilson@btopenworld.com
Page **55**.

Circus Architects
020 7953 7322
Pages **19b**, **36bl**.

Dive Architects
www.divearchitects.com
Pages **26l**, **40r**, **51l**.

Dominic Ash Ltd
tel/fax: 020 7689 0676
dominic@dominicash.co.uk
Pages **9**, **14**, **25b**.

Emma Bowman Interior Design
020 7622 2592
Emmabowman@yahoo.co.uk
Pages **10r**, **29**.

Fiona McLean, Architect
McLean Quinlan
020 8767 1633
Pages **38–39**.

Gustavo Martinez Design
+ 1 212 686 3102
gmdecor@aol.com
Pages **41l**, **49**.

Imogen Chappel
07803 156081
Pages **6–7**.

Jane Wellman
A hand-crafter of teddy bears
020 8275 0693
Page **1**.

Jessica Zoob
Artist
www.jessicazoob.com
Page **45**.

Josephine Macrander
Interior Designer
+ 31 20 6428100
Page **37l**.

jwflowers.com
www.jwflowers.com
Pages **52bl**, **58bl**.

Knott Architects
www.knottarchitects.co.uk
Page **19a**.

KRD – Kitchen Rogers Design
020 8944 7088
ab@krd.demon.co,uk
Pages **12r**, **59br**.

Kristiina Ratia Designs
+ 1 203 852 0027
Pages **24b**, **50**.

Littman Goddard Hogarth
www.lgh-architects.co.uk
Pages **33a**, **44l**, **47ar**.

Malin Iovino Design
020 7252 3542
iovino@btinternet.com
Pages **8r**, **40l**.

Marisa Tadiotto Cavalli
+ 39 02 36 51 14 49
marisacavalli@hotmail.com
Page **37ar**.

Moneo Brock Studio
www.moneobrock.com
Pages **28b**, **44r**.

Nico Rensch, Architeam
07711 412898
Pages **18**, **42**, **52r**.

Sage Wimer Coombe Architects
+ 1 212 226 9600
Pages **15l**, **48l**, **53l**.

Seth Stein, Architect
020 8968 8581
Page **20l**, **33b**.

Sharland & Lewis
www.sharlandandlewis.com
Pages **34b**, **46b**.

**Architect Simon Colebrook of the
Douglas Stephen Partnership**
www.dspl.co.uk
Pages **21**, **43l**, **53br**.

Steven Learner Studio
www.stevenlearnerstudio.com
Pages **32–33**.

Susie Atkinson Design
07768 814 134
Page **35**.

The Swedish Chair
www.theswedishchair.com
Page **52ar**.

Vanessa Arbuthnott
www.vanessaarbuthnott.co.uk
Page **46b**.

index

Italics indicate picture captions.

accessorizing
    babies' rooms *11*, 13
    bathrooms *57*
attic rooms *20*

babies' bedrooms 8–13
bathrooms 54–59
bedlinen
    for babies 10
    for boys 28
    for girls 18
bedrooms
    for babies 8–13
    for boys 22–29
    for girls 14–21
    shared 30–35
beds
    for boys *22, 24–25, 26*
    for girls *16–17*
    platform *19, 24*
boys' bedrooms 22–29

canopies *16, 17*
clothes storage
    for babies 12
    for boys 25–26
colour
    in babies' rooms 11
    in bathrooms 57
    in boys' rooms *25, 29*
    in girls' rooms 15, 20
    in play spaces 44
cots 10

dormitory theme *31*

eating spaces 48–53

fabrics (play spaces) 43, 45
fads 27
flooring
    in bathrooms *54, 57*
    in boys' rooms 26–27
    in eating spaces 53
    in play spaces 46

furniture
    for babies 10–11
    for boys *22*, 24–25
    for eating spaces *49*, 50
    for girls 18–20
    for play spaces 44–45

girls' bedrooms 14–21

highchairs 50

island units 50, *51*

kitchens 50–51

lighting
    babies' rooms 12
    boys' rooms 28
    girls' rooms *19*
living spaces
    bathrooms 54–59
    eating spaces 48–53
    play spaces 40–47

murals *34*, 35

nappy changing 11
nurseries 8–13

play spaces 40–47

safety (babies' rooms) 13
shared bedrooms 30–35
space, reorganizing 42
storage
    for babies *8*, 11, 12
    in bathrooms *57*
    for boys 24–26
    for girls 18–20, *20*
    in play spaces 43, *45*

tableware 51
tree mural *34*

wall treatments (bathrooms) 57
window dressings (babies' rooms) *11*